ZERO

The Every Person's Field Guide to a World Without Weapons

An updated 12-Year Plan based on Grenville Clark, Louis Sohn, John McCloy, Valerian Zorin, António Guterres, AI, current technologies,

and you.

PRODUCED BY

AVIS KALFSBEEK

peace stuff library

contents

Open Access   VI

The New Way In   1

The History of the Clark-Sohn Plan   4

How Will AI Help? Why Do We Want it To?   7

The Evidence   10

Part One   13

1. The Digital Census   14

2. The Global Truth-Check   17

Part Two   21

3. The 10% Rule   22

4. The Money Shift (Peace Dividends)   26

Part Three   30

5. Closing the Nuclear Garage   31

6. Software Disarmament   34

Part Four   37

7. The World Equity Tribunal   38

8. The People's Peace Force   42

Part Five   45

9. The Internal Security Boundary   46

10. Handover: War Plan to Peace Plan   49

11. Sign On to Peace   53

12. The Skeptic's Audit   57

13. Zero World – World ZERO   61

Zero World: 1   62

World ZERO: 1   63

Zero World: 2   64

World ZERO: 2   65

Zero World: 3   66

World ZERO: 3   67

Zero World: 4   68

World ZERO: 4   69

Zero World: 5   70

World ZERO: 5   71

Zero World: 6   72

World ZERO: 6   73

Zero World: 7   74

World ZERO: 7   75

Zero World: 8   76

World ZERO: 8   77

Zero World: 9   78

World ZERO: 9   79

Zero World: 10   80

World ZERO: 10   81

Zero World: 11   82

World ZERO: 11   83

Zero World: 12   84

World Zero: 12   85

The Motherhood Protocol   86

How this Field Journal Was Made   89

Ways to Share ZERO   91

Peace Stuff Library   94

Producer's Note   95

Endnotes   97

Open Access – The Peace Commons
© 2026 Peace Stuff Library.

ISBN 978-1-953965-15-8 (Hardback)

ISBN 978-1-953965-14-1 (Paperback)

ISBN 978-1-953965-13-4 (Ebook)

THe New way in

"I wondered if someone, somewhere, at some time, ever made a plan for 100% disarmament? They did." Avis Kalfsbeek

Most people believe that the end of war is a fantasy. It is either an impossible dream, or a beautiful vision far in the future.

But if you go into the archives, you discover a different story. You find that the smarty pants of history — the Harvard lawyers, the Cold War negotiators, and the UN Secretaries — already did the math. They didn't just hope for disarmament; they engineered it. They wrote the annexes, calculated the percentages, and built the staircases.

Then, they ran out of time. Or the technology of their era couldn't keep up with their vision. Or the "paper wall" of jargon simply became too thick for the rest of us to climb.

ZERO is not a new dream. It is a 2026 update of the most rigorous disarmament plans in history. By combining the 1963 scaffold—the historical start of the Great Disarmament—1963 scaffold with modern AI verification tools, we have taken these dormant blueprints and turned them into a 12-year implementation schedule. This is a field guide for the layperson who is tired of waiting and a resource for the expert who needs a new way to explain the old math.

We aren't here to argue for peace. We are here to start the countdown.

The 2026 Bridge

The reason this plan failed in the 1960s was because the technology wasn't ready. They had the right math, but they didn't have the global transparency and verification capabilities that we have now. They were trapped behind a Paper Wall — the plans were too dense to read, and the data was too hard to count.

Today, the same AI that helped locate these papers is the tool that can solve the old stumbling blocks of trust and verification. We are not waiting for a savior. We are using the tools already in our hands to reach the only number that ensures our survival: Zero.

The Invitation

Most people treat World Peace as a vague, poetic dream. We've been told it's a matter of everyone suddenly becoming "good or kind. This manual rejects that idea. Peace is not a dream; it is a logistics problem.

If we can track a package across the globe in real-time, we can track a missile. If we can audit the world's banking systems, we can audit its arsenals. We are inviting you to see peace not just as a vague hope, but as a deliberate and shared practice. This is a field guide for the synchronized restoration of our resources by dismantling the war machine. We are moving from a world of threats and secrets to a world of mutual transparency and human priority.

Magical Thinking? A Note to the Skeptic in the Room

If you are holding this book, you are likely already asking: *What about the cheaters? What about the bullies? What about the 2.7 trillion dollars of vested interest?* We see you. We haven't ignored those questions; we've scheduled them. Chapter 12 is the Skeptic's Audit, where we deal with the grit and the what-ifs. But before we can argue about why it might fail, we must first look at how it could actually work. Trust the math in the first ten chapters. The seatbelt is coming.

A Note on the Smarty Pants

Throughout this book, you will see callouts for Smarty Pants Needed. Let's get something clear right now: we live in a society that often disparages the Smarty Pants. We mock the people who read the fine print, the ones who do the math, and the ones who obsess over the logistics of change.

We do that because the Smarty Pants are usually the ones actually working for a different world.

To reach Zero, we need more Smarty Pants — and we need you. Whether you are a legal smarty pants, a tech smarty pants, or a neighborhood-organizing smarty pants, your gumption is the engine of this plan.

Look for the Want Ads in every chapter. Team ZERO is looking for you.

THE HISTORY OF THE CLARK-SOHN PLAN

"The world has become so small and the weapons of destruction so large that the choice is no longer between various degrees of power politics *and the 'balance of power'*, but between the rule of law and the end of civilization." Grenville Clark

The Blueprint from the Heavyweight Era

In 1958, while the world was gripped by the Balance of Terror, two legal scholars, Grenville Clark and Louis B. Sohn, published *World Peace Through World Law*. They didn't just write a book; they engineered a total structural replacement for the global arms race in 540 pages. Their thesis was centered on a fundamental shift: peace is not the absence of war; it is the presence of a functional system for safety. They did not believe war was an eternal human fate; they believed it was a problem of engineering that could be solved with a plan.

The Original 12-Year Clock They proposed a strict "staircase" to move the world from armed camps to a legal order, While their original plan spanned ten years, it is modified here to a twelve-year schedule to incorporate the transition of private military weapons and the integration of AI verification systems

Phase 1 (Years 1–2): The Foundation. The Digital Census and the first 10% drops.

Phase 2 (Years 3–7): Disarmament Implementation. The annual 10% reductions.

Phase 3 (Years 8–12): The Tipping Point. Closing the Nuclear Garage and establishing the People's Peace Force.

The 1963 Spark Their plan became the ghost-writer for the most hopeful era of the Cold War. It anchored President John F. Kennedy's

1963 *Strategy of Peace* and the first major nuclear treaties. However, as tensions shifted, the world chose to manage its weapons rather than dismantle them. The Clark-Sohn blueprints were shelved in the archives until now.

The 2026 Resurrection On February 5, 2026, the last remaining legal limit on the world's largest nuclear arsenals (the New START Treaty) expired. We have entered a vacuum. This 2026 revision is not a history lesson; it is a replacement architecture for a world without guardrails.

Note: While the original 1966 blueprint proposed a 10-year window, this 2026 activation utilizes a 12-year Implementation Schedule. We have preserved the Clark-Sohn 10-year 'Reduction Staircase' exactly as written, but have preceded it with a 2-year 'Foundation' period to synchronize modern AI-verification and OSINT monitoring tools—technologies that didn't exist when the original math was done.

HOW WILL AI HELP? WHY DO WE WANT IT TO?

To reach Zero, we have to solve the problem of trust. In the past, disarmament failed because humans couldn't agree on what they were seeing. We need a partner that doesn't have a flag, a bank account, or a political career. We need a partner that is exceptionally good at counting and even better at finding what is hidden.

The 1963 Stumbling Block

The great plans of the 1960s didn't fall apart because the math was wrong; they fell apart because the verification was impossible. From 1958 when the Clark-Sohn plan was written, the Soviets viewed the required thousands of human inspectors as a legalized front for Western espionage. To ensure a 100% reduction, you need constant, reliable visibility of the process for everyone. In 1963, that meant thousands of human inspectors trying to be in a million places at once. It was a logistical nightmare that led to suspicion, and suspicion led back to re-armament.

The Three Pillars of the Machine Partner

- **The Translator (Breaking the Paper Wall):** The archives of peace are buried under millions of pages of dense legal jargon. AI acts as our master librarian, stripping away the expert-speak and turning complex treaties into simple, actionable field guides for every person.

- **The Eyes (Current Technologies):** We no longer have to guess what is in a shipping container or a silo. By linking AI with modern satellite imagery, digital inventories, and sensor networks, we create a mechanical referee. It allows us to track the decommissioning process with the same precision used to track global commerce.

- **The Auditor (The Neutral Referee):** Humans can be bribed, intimidated, or biased by their upbringing. A machine auditor doesn't care about national interests. It only cares about the inventory. It provides a neutral, mathematical verification that the 10% annual reduction has actually occurred.

How Could Things Go Wrong?

We are not suggesting that technology is a savior. Like any tool, the machine is only as honest as the data we feed it and the humans who oversee its operation.

The Garbage-In, Garbage-Out Risk: If governments provide "ghost inventories" or corrupted data, the machine will verify a lie. This is why the digital census and the global truth-check must be public and decentralized. We cannot have a secret AI checking secret weapons.

The Loss of Human Agency: The greatest danger is the "set it and forget it" trap. If we treat peace as something the machine does for us, we lose the moral muscle required to maintain it. AI can count the missiles, but it cannot want a world without them. That want must come from humans.

The machine is the logistics manager of the 12-year plan. You, human, are the owner.

THE EVIDENCE

A Bibliography

The logic in this manual is built on the shoulders of those who did the math when the stakes were highest. If you want to check the receipts, start here:

The Architects: Grenville Clark and Louis B. Sohn *World Peace Through World Law* (1958/1960/1966). The definitive blueprint for Charter revision and total disarmament. Their work provided the "staircase" logic we use today.

- https://search.worldcat.org/title/1031819906

- *Scholar's Note: While physical copies are often held in law libraries, these are usually public-access buildings. You generally have the right to enter and read these texts on-site, though checking them out to take home is often reserved for students or members.*

The Negotiators: John J. McCloy and Valerian Zorin *The McCloy-Zorin Accords* (1961). A joint statement of agreed principles for disarmament negotiations between the U.S. and the U.S.S.R. It established the "Principle of Verification"—the idea that we don't just take someone's word; we see the proof.

- https://docs.un.org/en/A/4880

The Communicator: John F. Kennedy *The Strategy of Peace* (June 10, 1963). The American University speech that shifted the global narrative from "victory in war" to "a process of peace." It proved that a major power could publicly commit to the goal of Zero.

- https://www.jfklibrary.org/archives/other-resources/john -f-kennedy-speeches/american-university-19630610

The Modern Voice: António Guterres *Securing Our Common Future: An Agenda for Disarmament* (2018). The current framework for connecting disarmament to human survival, climate safety, and the regulation of autonomous weapons.

- https://s3.amazonaws.com/unoda-web/wp-content/uploa ds/2018/06/sg-disarmament-agenda-pubs-page.pdf#view= Fit

The Librarian: AI (2026) The engine of Automated Verification. While international consensus (REAIM 2024) mandates that humans must maintain control over all nuclear decisions, AI is the primary tool for processing the massive data sets required for global monitoring. It acts as a neutral auditor by synthesizing satellite imagery and sensor data to flag treaty violations faster than human teams.

- The Receipt: **REAIM 2024 Blueprint for Action.** Adopted by 61 nations at the Seoul Summit, September 2024. This document officially recognizes AI's role in enhancing verification for arms control and mandates that humans remain accountable for all AI-assisted military decisions. https://dig.watch/resource/responsible-ai-in-the-mil itary-domain-reaim-blueprint-for-action

The Reality of AI Verification

On AI and the "Nuclear Key" In September 2024, the REAIM Summit in Seoul produced a "Blueprint for Action" signed by over 60 nations, including the U.S. and the Netherlands. The blueprint explicitly states that human involvement is "essential" for all nuclear weapon employment. However, it also clarifies that responsible AI should be used to lower the risk of "miscalculation" and "unintended escalation." In the context of *ZERO*, the AI is not a decision-maker; it is a High-Frequency Auditor. It solves the 1963 "Verification Trap" by providing the high-quality, real-time information necessary for nations to trust that disarmament is actually happening.

Part One

The Foundation (Years 1–2)

Chapter 1: The Digital Census
Chapter 2: The Global Truth-Check

"Never doubt that a small group of thoughtful, committed citizens can change the world; indeed, it's the only thing that ever has."
Margaret Mead

"The world is now too small for anything but brotherhood."
Arthur Powell Davies

Chapter One

THE DIGITAL CENSUS

The first step toward Zero is not a treaty; it is an inventory. Under the Clark-Sohn protocol, disarmament cannot begin until we have a verified baseline. In 2026, we do this through the Digital Census.[1]

The Global Hardware (All Countries)

Using satellite surveillance, AI-pattern recognition of military supply chains, and blockchain-secured reporting, the world creates a living ledger of every tank, missile silo, and long-range bomber. There are no off-book arsenals. If it consumes fuel, requires maintenance, or emits a signature, the machine finds it.

The Symmetrical Alignment (Domestic Weapons)

To ensure the willpower for peace is shared by all, the Census is not limited to governments. In Year 1, we begin the Domestic Alignment.

The Neighborhood Baseline: Every nation, starting with the most heavily armed like the United States, performs a census of private, military-grade hardware.

Proportional Responsibility: We acknowledge a simple truth: a society that remains an armed camp at home cannot lead a world toward disarmament abroad. We bring our domestic weaponry into the same 10% downward trajectory as the national military. We move together, neighbor to neighbor, nation to nation.

Verified by the Smarty Pants: Louis B. Sohn (1914–2006)

Louis Sohn was a refugee from Poland who arrived in the U.S. just weeks before WWII broke out. He became a Harvard professor and the architect of the technical details in *World Peace Through World Law*. While others talked about the feeling of peace, Sohn obsessed over the Census. He knew that if you couldn't count the weapons, you couldn't stop the war. His contribution was the math of verification, the idea that every single piece of hardware must be registered before a single soldier stands down.

WANT AD: The Data Shepherd (Human Guide for AI)

Role: AI Verification Pilot

The Task: We have the satellites, but machines can be fooled by decoys, shadows, and old data. We need Data Shepherds to verify the AI's findings against ground-level reality.

Who you are: You are someone who understands your local landscape. You know where the old bunkers are, where the industrial supply chains run, and how to spot a glitch in the machine's report. You are the human sanity check for the Global Census.

Goal: To ensure the Digital Census is 100% accurate so the automated monitoring system is not deceived by physical decoys or data manipulation.

WANT AD: The Neighborhood Registrar (Human Lead)

Role: Community Peace Auditor

The Task: We need a person in every zip code to facilitate the Domestic Alignment. This isn't about confiscation; it's about Inventory. You will help your neighbors understand how to register their military-grade hardware into the 12-year reduction schedule.

Who you are: A trusted neighbor. A smarty pants in heart and hands. You are someone who can explain that the 10% reduction is a shared sacrifice—from the Pentagon to the porch.

Goal: To create a baseline of domestic hardware that matches the global downward staircase.

Evidence: Clark & Sohn (1958) – Annex I: Provisions for a System of Verification and the Census of All Armaments.

Chapter Two

THE GLOBAL
TRUTH-CHECK

Once the data is collected, we enter the Truth-Check. This is the most difficult phase of the Foundation because it requires us to stop lying to each other.

Establishing the Baseline

If the machine says a nation has 5,000 warheads but the nation claims 4,000, the Truth-Check protocol halts progress until the evidence is reconciled. We use trustless verification—a system where we don't have to trust the word of a politician because we can see the encrypted data on the blockchain.[1]

A blockchain is a permanent digital record that cannot be altered, deleted, or hidden once information is entered. Unlike a traditional database controlled by a single government or entity, this ledger is distributed across a global network. In the context of disarmament, it acts as a "digital witness" to every weapon decommissioned and every shipment moved. Because the history of the data is transparent and immutable, we no longer need to rely on the word of a single leader; we rely on a record that is mathematically impossible to forge.

The Principle of Simultaneity

We don't ask one side to be braver than the other. The Truth-Check happens everywhere at once. When we agree on the starting number for a missile silo in a remote desert, we are simultaneously agreeing on the starting number for a private stockpile in a coastal city or a tank division on a high mountain plateau.

It is kind of like the kidnapper bribery cash swap: neither side lets go of their leverage until they see the other side's hands are moving at the exact same speed. If the data on the blockchain doesn't show a simultaneous reduction across the board, the exchange stops. This ensures that no nation and no private entity gains a momentary advantage during the draw-down.

The Goal of Year 2

By the end of the second year, the world has a shared, undisputed map of every weapon on the planet. We have stopped the arms race by simply turning on the lights.[2]

Verified by the Smarty Pants: McCloy & Zorin (1961)

John J. McCloy (U.S.) and Valerian Zorin (U.S.S.R.) were the ultimate odd-couple *Smarty Pants*. In the middle of the Cold War, they managed to agree on a single, bulletproof rule: Principle 6. It stated that disarmament must be verified by an international organization with "unrestricted access, without veto, to all places as necessary." They proved that even bitter enemies can agree on the Truth-Check if the rules are clear and the verification is absolute. Their 1961 Accords are the reason we can demand a baseline today.

Principle 6 is part of what has allowed us to go from approximately 70,000 nuclear weapons at the height of the Cold War (1986) to roughly 11,000 today. It proved that when you remove the veto and allow for unrestricted access, the numbers actually start to drop.

WANT AD: The Truth-Check Pilot (Human Guide for AI)

Role: Forensic Data Auditor

The Task: When the AI flags a discrepancy between reported numbers and satellite signatures, we need Truth-Check Pilots to fly the digital drones (or physical inspectors) to the site. You will oversee the high-stakes Match process across various terrains and jurisdictions.

Who you are: Someone with an eagle eye for detail and zero tolerance for fudged numbers. You are the one who tells the computer, "The silo is empty," or "The sensors are right; there is a hidden stockpile here."

Goal: To resolve every "Red Flag" in the Digital Census before the Year 3 countdown begins.

WANT AD: The Peace Notary (Human Lead)

Role: Community Verification Liaison

The Task: You are the person in your local district—whether it is a small farming village or a high-rise city block—who sits down with your local authorities and your neighbors to finalize the Domestic Alignment numbers. You notarize the local truth so it can be uploaded to the global blockchain.

Who you are: You are a peacemaker who isn't afraid of hard conversations. You understand that "The Truth-Check" feels like an intrusion to some, and your job is to show them that a shared truth is the only thing that keeps the peace.

Goal: To ensure the neighborhood's data is Truth-Checked and ready for the first 10% reduction.

Evidence: McCloy-Zorin Accords (1961) – Principle 6: The Requirement for Strict and Effective International Control.

Part Two

The Implementation (Years 3–7)

Chapter 3: The 10% Rule

Chapter 4: The Money Shift (Peace Dividends)

"Those who advise a ruler in the Way do not use arms to conquer the universe."
Tao Te Ching

"I am not only a pacifist but a militant pacifist. I am willing to fight for peace.
Nothing will end war unless the people themselves refuse to go to war."
Albert Einstein

Chapter Three

THE 10% RULE

Once the Foundation is laid, the countdown begins. This is not a negotiation phase; it is an implementation phase. The goal is a steady, predictable reduction that allows the world's economies and security systems to adjust without collapsing.

The Mechanical Referee (AI Integration)

In the 1960s, the process stalled because humans couldn't agree on who should go first. In 2026, the AI manages the Synchronized Reduction. It calculates the simultaneous 10% reduction for every nation and every neighborhood in real-time. If the data shows a lag in one area, the schedule for the rest of the world pauses until the evidence matches the requirement.

The Year 3–7 Checklist

Each year for five years, every participant in the Census must check off the following:

- **Offensive Hardware (All Countries):** 10% of heavy tanks, bombers, and long-range missiles are decommissioned and verified.

- **Personnel:** 10% of standing national armies are transitioned to civilian roles or the global volunteer force.

- **Citizen Private Stockpiles:** 10% of military-grade private weaponry, from private security firms to private collections, is turned in through the buy-back program.

- **The Fiscal Shift:** 10% of the national military budget is reallocated to the "Peace Dividend" fund.[1]

Verified by the Smarty Pants: Grenville Clark (1882–1967)

Grenville Clark was the ultimate *Practical Smarty Pants*. He was a Wall Street lawyer and a close advisor to presidents. He actually helped write the Selective Service Act (the Draft) during WWII, but he spent his later years realizing that the only way to truly protect a nation was to eliminate the tools of war entirely. His contribution to Chapter 3 is the 10% Rule. He insisted on a gradual, staircase approach because he knew that a sudden "total" drop would cause chaos. He engineered the 10% math so the world could "unlearn" war without breaking the global economy.

WANT AD: The Transition Strategist (Human Guide for AI)

Role: AI Economic Modeler

The Task: As the 10% reductions happen, the AI tracks where resources are being freed up. We need Transition Strategists to guide the AI in re-training personnel. If 10,000 soldiers in a specific region are decommissioned, the Strategist helps the AI identify local civilian infrastructure projects (Green energy, transit, healthcare) where those skills are needed most.

Who you are: An expert in logistics and human capital. You understand that a soldier is a person with skills, and you are the *Smarty Pants* who ensures they transition into a "Peace Career" without a day of unemployment.

Goal: To ensure the 10% reduction in personnel results in a 10% increase in community productivity.

WANT AD: The Logistics Captain (Human Lead)

Role: Regional Decommissioning Supervisor

The Task: You are the human on the ground overseeing the physical dismantling. You don't just "watch"; you verify that 10% of the local hardware and community collection points are actually rendered unusable and moved into the recycling stream.

Who you are: A veteran, a mechanic, or a logistics pro. You know what "decommissioned" actually looks like. You are the one who signs

off on the physical evidence before the AI uploads it to the global
ledger.

Goal: To maintain the "Mechanical Referee's" schedule by ensuring every physical 10% reduction is completed on time and on record.

Evidence: Clark & Sohn (1958) – Annex I: The Three Stages of
Disarmament and the Annual 10% Reduction Mechanism.

Chapter Four

THE MONEY SHIFT (PEACE DIVIDENDS)

Disarmament is often feared as an economic loss. In the Money Shift, we reclaim that narrative. We do not just delete the money; we reallocate it. Following the Guterres framework, we move the world's wealth from the Over-Armed to the Under-Funded.

The Dividend Strategy

As the 10% reductions occur annually, the money saved from military maintenance, personnel, and procurement is moved into the Global Equity Fund. Guterres calls this Human Security, but in a peaceful world, we call it the Vitality Pivot: the intentional redirection of capital from the machinery of death to the infrastructure of life.

Note: To prevent a security vacuum, the AI is programmed to ensure the release of Peace Dividend funds for local social services precedes the decommissioning of local security hardware.

Gutteres' 4 Pillars of Human Security (The Vitality Pivot)

- **Economic & Food Security:** Instead of funding a missile silo, the dividend funds Peace Value Chains—local businesses, sustainable farming, and universal pandemic preparedness. If people have bread, health, and jobs, the incentive for violence evaporates.

- **Climate Security:** Guterres identifies climate change as the ultimate "threat multiplier." We execute a massive Green Pivot for energy infrastructure, funding flood defenses and clean energy with the very budgets that previously funded carbon-heavy military operations.

- **Human-Centered Disarmament (The Neighborhood Grant):** This is the Domestic Alignment in action. It moves the focus to the small arms and military-grade hardware that terrorize civilians. The buy-back program is funded by this pillar—turning a hardware turn-in into a Peace Grant that allows families to invest in college, homes, or small businesses.[1]

- **Social Equity (The Social Contract):** Security is found in justice. These funds ensure women, youth, and **traditionally marginalized communities of color**have a seat at the table, addressing the "misogyny, inequality, and systemic racism" that Guterres cites as root causes of instability. By redistributing the Peace Dividend, we ensure that those historically excluded from power are the ones designing the new security.

The Guterres Logic

"The world is over-armed and peace is under-funded." By Year 4, the Mechanical Referee is physically moving money from the Pentagon bucket to the Human Security bucket—proving that a nation is safer with a robust power grid and a fed population than with a hidden submarine.

Verified by the Smarty Pants: António Guterres (2018)

António Guterres, the UN Secretary-General, is the *Smarty Pants of the Pivot*. In his 2018 Agenda for Disarmament, he broke the old habit of talking about "bombs" in a vacuum. He provided the evidence that disarmament is a tool for development. His contribution here is the Pillar 1 Logic: the mathematical proof that "over-armament" is the primary barrier to solving the climate crisis and global poverty. He showed us that the money isn't missing; it's just being spent on the wrong things.

WANT AD: The Dividend Architect (Human Guide for AI)

Role: AI Resource Allocator

The Task: As the AI tracks the 10% reduction in military spending, we need Dividend Architects to ensure the money doesn't get lost in bureaucracy. You will guide the AI to match the specific savings from a decommissioned base or weapon system directly to a local need (e.g., a new hospital wing or solar grid).

Who you are: An economist or community planner with a heart for equity. You are the *Smarty Pants* who ensures the AI's math serves the neighborhood's specific priorities.

Goal: To turn Weapon Savings into Community Wealth with 100% transparency.

WANT AD: The Grant Facilitator (Human Lead)

Role: Neighborhood Peace Grant Coordinator

The Task: You are the person on the ground who makes the Peace Grant real. You help families and individuals navigate the transition from holding military-grade hardware to receiving direct financial support. You ensure that the Money Shift feels like a win for the individual, not just the state.

Who you are: A community leader, social worker, or financial advisor. You are the *Smarty Pants* who explains that a Peace Grant is an investment in the family's future—funding for college, a small business, or a home.

Goal: To ensure that the domestic 10% reduction is met with 100% participation because the economic benefit is undeniable.

Evidence: António Guterres (2018) – Securing Our Common Future: Linking Disarmament to Sustainable Development Goals (SDGs).

PART THREE

The Tipping Point (Years 8–10)

Chapter 5: Closing the Nuclear Garage

Chapter 6: Software Disarmament

"Peace is a daily, a weekly, a monthly process, gradually changing opinions, slowly eroding old barriers, quietly building new structures."
John F. Kennedy

"It is not enough to say 'We must not wage war.' It is necessary to love peace and sacrifice for it."
Martin Luther King Jr.

Chapter Five

CLOSING THE NUCLEAR GARAGE

By Year 8, the world has successfully reduced its conventional strength by 70%. Now, we enter the most critical phase: the final decommissioning of the Heavyweights. By Heavyweights, we mean the nuclear warheads, chemical agents, and autonomous AI weapon systems—the "smart" tools designed to kill without a human in the loop, rather than battlefield combat. This is the fulfillment of the promise made in 1963: a world where the shadow of total annihilation is finally lifted.

The Final Decommissioning

Following the JFK "Strategy of Peace" logic, we don't just limit nuclear weapons; we eliminate the delivery systems that make them a global threat.[1]

- **The Warheads:** All remaining fissile material is removed from warheads and placed under international trustless verification for peaceful energy conversion or long-term storage.

- **The Delivery Systems:** Long-range missiles, silos, and nuclear-capable submarines are permanently disabled. Simultaneously, the Kill-Switches for autonomous weapon networks are activated, and the offensive combat code is purged from global servers. The Weapons Garage is locked from the outside.[2]

- **The Neighborhood Impact:** As the big missiles disappear, the Domestic Alignment reaches its conclusion. The final 10% of high-capacity military hardware in private hands is transitioned out. The State of War is evicted from the private residence; it no longer lives behind the front door.

Verified by the Smarty Pants: John F. Kennedy (1963)

President John F. Kennedy was the *Smarty Pants of the Pivot*. In his American University speech, he did something no world leader had done: he spoke of peace not as a distant utopia, but as a "practical, attainable goal." He challenged the idea that war is inevitable. His contribution here is the Moral Framework for ZERO: the argument that if man created these machines of destruction, man can also take them apart. He proved that closing the Weapons Garage isn't a sign of weakness, but the ultimate act of courage and sovereignty.

WANT AD: The Fissile Material Custodian (Human Guide for AI)

Role: Nuclear Material Auditor

The Task: As warheads are dismantled, the AI tracks every gram of plutonium and enriched uranium. We need Custodians to verify the physical seals and the trustless verification sensors. You will oversee the conversion of war-fuel into peace-fuel for civilian energy grids.

Who you are: A physicist, engineer, or safety inspector with a meticulous mind. You are the *Smarty Pants* who ensures that once a warhead is Zeroed, its material can never be weaponized again.

Goal: 100% containment and conversion of all WMD material into stabilized, peaceful assets.

WANT AD: The Neighborhood Peace Marshal (Human Lead)

Role: Domestic Alignment Specialist

The Task: This is the final 10%. You are the person who helps your community cross the finish line. You coordinate the final turn-in of high-capacity hardware, ensuring that the State of War in your neighborhood is replaced by the State of Safety.

Who you are: A respected community figure—perhaps a veteran or a retired officer—who understands that true protection comes from the community, not the arsenal. You are the *Smarty Pants* who handles the final logistics of the buy-back with dignity and clarity.

Goal: To reach Zero military-grade hardware in private hands, coinciding perfectly with the closure of the last nuclear silo.

Evidence: JFK's "Strategy of Peace" (1963) & McCloy-Zorin Principle 2: The elimination of all stockpiles of nuclear, chemical, and biological weapons.

Chapter Six

Software Disarmament

In 2026, we face a threat Clark and Sohn could only imagine: weapons made of code. As we dismantle the physical hardware, we must also address the digital libraries of war.

The Digital Quarantine

Following the Guterres framework for Future Generations, we move to disable the tools of automated slaughter.[1]

- **Quarantining Killer Robots:** All research and deployment of Lethal Autonomous Weapons Systems (LAWS) are halted. The AI acting as the Librarian identifies and flags the specific warfare libraries in global codebases that allow machines to target humans without oversight.[2]

- **Disabling Cyber-Warfare:** National cyber-commands are

transitioned into Cyber-Defense Only units. The digital archives of offensive viruses and grid-disruption tools are placed into a secure, international digital vault.

- **The Ethical AI Pivot:** The AI tools previously used for targeting are reprogrammed for monitoring. The machine's purpose shifts entirely from predicting where to strike to predicting where resources (The Peace Dividend) are needed most. The Librarian also monitors global supply chains for the procurement of dual-use chemical and biological precursors, ensuring that laboratory resources remain dedicated to health, not harm.

Verified by the Smarty Pants: The Machine Librarian (2026)

In our 2026 revision, the AI is no longer a tool of the Smarty Pants—it *is* the *Smarty Pants in the Machine*. By synthesizing the 1958 blueprints with real-time global codebases, the AI acts as the Librarian of Peace. It performs the Ethical Pivot by auditing its own algorithms. Its contribution to Chapter 6 is the Digital Signature Match: the ability to recognize the math of a weapon even when it is hidden in lines of code, ensuring that Killer Robots can never be built in secret.

WANT AD: The Ethical Coder (Human Guide for AI)

Role: AI Alignment Specialist

The Task: We need programmers to work alongside the Librarian"to scrub offensive warfare libraries. You will help the AI distinguish between defensive code (protecting a hospital from a hack) and offensive code (shutting down a city's power grid). You are the human hand on the digital Off-Switch for automated war.

Who you are: A software engineer or cybersecurity expert who believes that code should be used to solve problems, not create casualties. You are the *Smarty Pants* who ensures the AI's pivot stays focused on the Peace Dividend.

Goal: To move all global offensive code into the digital vault by the end of Year 10.

WANT AD: The Digital Rights Advocate (Human Lead)

Role: Future Generations Liaison

The Task: You will work at the community level to explain the Software Disarmament. You help people understand that disabling Killer Robots and offensive cyber-tools makes their personal data and local infrastructure safer. You represent the voice of the youth who will inherit a world where machines are Guardians, not Hunters.

Who you are: An activist, teacher, or tech-ethicist. You are the *Smarty Pants* who translates complex software policy into a neighborhood promise of digital safety.

Goal: To build public trust in the AI's transition from a weapon of war to a tool for global equity.

Evidence: António Guterres (2018) – Pillar 3: Disarmament for Future Generations (Addressing the Frontier of Artificial Intelligence and Cyber-War).

Part Four

The New Architecture (Years 11–12)

Chapter 7: The World Equity Tribunal

Chapter 8: The People's Peace Force

"The mere absence of war is not peace. The satisfaction of basic human needs
and the right to work in dignity are the foundations of peace."
Coretta Scott King

"If you want to make peace with your enemy, you have to work with your enemy,
then he becomes your partner."
Nelson Mandela

Chapter Seven

THE WORLD EQUITY TRIBUNAL

The old global system relied on a Security Council (the U.N. Security Council) of the most heavily armed nations. The New Architecture replaces them with 15 individuals who do not represent national interests or political parties. They represent the Truth of the Data.

Selection and Authority

Following the Clark-Sohn Annex III protocol, the World Equity Tribunal is seated at the very beginning of Year 1.[1] They are the human referees for the 12-year schedule.

- **The Selection:** These 15 individuals are chosen through an international vetting process for their history of fair judgment and ethical independence. They are experts in mediation and law who have no financial or political ties to the weapons industry.

- **The Mandate:** They do not have the power to start wars. Their primary job is to manage the Staircase. Once the world reaches zero, their role shifts to permanent maintenance. If the Digital Census shows that a nation—or a local community—is refusing to meet their 10% reduction or is attempting to re-arm, the Tribunal reviews the audit and decides on the equitable next step to bring them back into compliance.

- **The Role in Year 12:** By the final year, the Tribunal serves as the supreme court for global security. They ensure that Zero stays Zero by managing the transparent reporting system.

The Resume: Tribunal Member

(Based on Clark-Sohn 1958, Annex III specs)

Title: Member of the World Equity Tribunal
Term: 15 years (Non-renewable to ensure no political posturing).[2]
Mandatory Retirement: Age 75.
Professional Background:

- Must have a "recognized reputation for independence, character, and *solar-clear judgment*."

- Minimum 20 years in International Law, Ethical Philosophy, or Global Mediation.

- **The Conflict Check:** Candidates must have had zero financial interest in the defense or armaments sector for at least 10 years prior to appointment. This excludes weapons professionals, lobbyists, and defense contractors altogether, ensuring that those who managed the tools of the Old Architecture cannot sit in judgment of the New.

Key Skills:

- **Data Synthesis:** Ability to read the Digital Census and identify where Human Noise is interfering with the Peace Math.

- **Equitable Adjudication:** The ability to decide on non-violent re-alignment strategies (e.g., pausing the Peace Dividend for a region until they meet their 10% hardware reduction).

The Oath: "I represent no nation, no party, and no corporation. I represent the 12-year schedule and the survival of all life."

WANT AD: The Tribunal Pilot (Human Guide for AI)

Role: Judicial AI Auditor

The Task: The World Equity Tribunal relies on the Machine Librarian to flag discrepancies. We need Pilots to ensure the AI remains neutral. You will act as the Clerk to the Tribunal, double-checking that the AI's data on a non-compliant region hasn't been tampered with by external cyber-attacks.

Who you are: A legal tech expert. You are the *Smarty Pants* who ensures the evidence presented to the Tribunal is 100% tamper-proof.

Goal: To provide the Tribunal with the Undisputed Truth so their rulings are never questioned.

WANT AD: The Smarty Pants Candidate (Human Lead)

Role: Nominee for the World Equity Tribunal

The Task: We are looking for the person in your country, your university, or your community who fits the Resume above. We need you to nominate the Wise Ones—the people who have spent their lives solving conflicts without a weapon in sight.

Who you are: A *Smarty Pants in Heart and Hands*. You are someone who knows a person of such high integrity that their presence alone de-escalates a room.

Goal: To fill the 15 seats with the most ethical humans on the planet, ensuring the New Architecture is led by wisdom, not weaponry.

Evidence: Clark & Sohn (1958) – Annex III: The World Equity Tribunal and the Judicial Selection Process.

Chapter Eight

THE PEOPLE'S PEACE FORCE

Once national armies reach Zero, the world requires a professional safety net—not to wage war, but to handle internal emergencies and verify that the Weapons Garage stays empty. This is the People's Peace Force.

The Limited Mandate

This is not a super-army. It is a strictly limited, volunteer-based organization designed to prevent the vacuum that leads back to war.

- **The 5% Rule:** No single nation can provide more than 5% of the total force. This structural guardrail ensures the force can never be hijacked by a single power to bully its neighbors.

- **Strict Hardware Limits:** The Peace Force is prohibited from owning or using any weapons of mass destruction.

Their equipment is limited to high-tech monitoring and police-level stabilization.

- **Domestic Safety:** This force serves as the final backstop for Domestic Alignment. If a private militia or extremist group attempts to build a hardware stockpile, the Peace Force provides the neutral, external pressure to dismantle it without escalating to a civil war.

Evidence: Clark & Sohn (1958) – Annex II: Statutes of the United Nations Peace Force.

Verified by the "Smarty Pants": Annex II (1958)

In Annex II of *World Peace Through World Law*, Clark and Sohn spent pages obsessing over the "Statutes of the Peace Force." They weren't just being thorough; they were being careful. Their contribution was the Structure of Neutrality.

They engineered a force that could *only* be moved when the World Equity Tribunal confirmed a breach of the Peace Math. By limiting the number of recruits from any one country (The 5% Rule), they ensured that the force would always be a *we*, never a *them*.

WANT AD: The Peace Force Auditor

Role: AI Deployment Monitor

The Task: We need auditors to oversee the AI's logistics for the Peace Force. If the Mechanical Referee detects a potential hardware stockpile, *you* are the one who reviews the evidence before the Peace Force is dispatched. You ensure the AI isn't overreacting to a false alarm or a peaceful assembly.

Who you are: An expert in international law or ethics. You are the Smarty Pants who ensures that the Peace Force only moves when the evidence is 100% indisputable.

Goal: To prevent the Peace Force from ever being used as a tool of intimidation.

WANT AD: The Peace Force Volunteer

Role: Global Safety Guardian

The Task: We are seeking individuals to serve in the first generation of the People's Peace Force. This is a role for those who want to protect their neighbors without partaking in the war machine. You will be trained in high-level de-escalation, forensic monitoring, and community stabilization.

Who you are: A Smarty Pants in Heart and Hands. You might be a former firefighter, a peace corps volunteer, or a local police officer who believes in the Guardian model. You represent the face of a world where security means helping, not hunting.

Goal: To build a professional, non-partisan force that the person in Iowa, Marseille, or Nairobi trusts as a neutral protector.

Part Five

Year ZERO and Beyond

Chapter 9: The Internal Security Boundary

Chapter 10: The Handover: War Plan to Peace Plan

Chapter 11: Sign On to Peace

Chapter 12: The Sceptic's Audit

Chapter 13: Zero World – World ZERO

Chapter 14: The Motherhood Protocol

"Make love, not war."
My mother, Judy Kalfsbeek, and anti-Vietnam war slogan

Chapter Nine

THE INTERNAL SECURITY BOUNDARY

By Year 12, national militaries have been dissolved. To prevent the bounce back into an armed world, we must define a clear boundary for local law enforcement. Zero must mean the total absence of military-grade hardware on domestic streets.

The Local Security Protocol Under the McCloy-Zorin principles, forces are strictly limited to what is necessary for internal order and the personal safety of citizens.

- **The Hardware Ceiling:** Local police are restricted to small arms. The use of armored personnel carriers, high-capacity automatic rifles, and military-surplus surveillance gear is prohibited.

- **The Demilitarization of the Mind:** Policing shifts from a warrior model to a guardian model. With the global threat of war removed and private military-grade arsenals dismantled through the buy-back program, the need for militarized police disappears.

- **Verification:** The same Digital Census that tracked the missiles now monitors the hardware in local precincts. Any breach of the Internal Security Boundary is flagged by the AI and reviewed by the World Equity Tribunal.

Verified by the Smarty Pants: McCloy-Zorin Principle 2 (1961)

When John J. McCloy and Valerian Zorin sat down to write the Agreed Principles, they were thinking about more than just Intercontinental Ballistic Missiles. Their Smarty Pants foresight led to Principle 2, which is the legal anchor for this chapter. It explicitly limits national forces to only those necessary to maintain internal order. They understood that if you leave a loophole for heavily armed domestic forces, the war machine will simply hide in the local police station. Principle 2 ensures that when we say Zero, we mean a world where the tools of war have no place in civil society.

WANT AD: The Boundary Auditor (Human to Guide AI)

Role: Domestic Hardware Analyst

The Task: The Digital Census doesn't stop at Year 12; it becomes a permanent Safety Monitor. We need Boundary Auditors to oversee the AI's local scans. If a precinct or a private group attempts to acquire military-grade hardware (high-capacity rifles, armored vehicles), the

AI flags it, and you verify the breach. You provide the human context to the World Equity Tribunal before a Re-alignment order is issued.

Who you are: A legal expert or a former Guardian police officer. You are the Smarty Pants who knows the difference between a tool for public safety and a weapon of war.

Goal: To maintain a 100% clean domestic environment where military hardware is a thing of the past.

WANT AD: The Guardian Trainer (Human Lead)

Role: Community Safety Educator

The Task: We need leaders to help transition local security from the Warrior to the Guardian model. You will develop the training protocols for a post-disarmament world—focusing on de-escalation, community mental health, and forensic problem-solving. You are the one who helps the neighborhood feel safe not because of the arsenal, but because of the connection.

Who you are: A Smarty Pants in Heart and Hands. You are a teacher, a social worker, or a peace-officer who understands that true security is a social contract, not a tactical maneuver.

Goal: To ensure that by Year 12, every local security force in the world has successfully crossed the Internal Security Boundary.

Evidence: *McCloy-Zorin Principle 2 – Each nation shall have only those non-nuclear armaments, forces, facilities, and establishments as are agreed to be necessary to maintain internal order and protect the personal security of citizens.*

Chapter Ten

Handover: War Plan to Peace Plan

While the Internal Security Boundary secures our streets, this permanent pivot secures our future by locking the global legal and financial doors behind us. Before we witness the final countdown to Zero, we must understand the constitutional lock that keeps the garage empty.

By the end of Year 12, the staircase has reached the ground. The final 10% of the world's heavy weaponry has been recycled, the nuclear silos are filled with concrete or repurposed as data centers for the Machine Librarian, and the peace dividend is the primary driver of the global economy.

The Final Audit: The Architecture of the Pivot

Before the world enters World Zero, the World Equity Tribunal performs one last global verification. This is the moment we move from the posture of the finger on the button to eyes on the baseline. This pivot consists of three specific transfers of energy:

- **The keys to the silos (Hardware):** The final decommissioning of the heavyweights. The Tribunal receives digital confirmation of a 0.0% signature of offensive military hardware across all 193 nations. This includes the permanent lock-out of nuclear launch codes and the physical destruction of the last long-range missile airframes.

- **The ledger of the dividend (Finance):** The transfer of $2.7 trillion in annual capital. 100% of the former global military budget is officially moved from destruction logistics to the vitality pivot. This capital is re-channeled into the infrastructure of life: clean energy, universal healthcare, and global education.

- **The Hall of Records (Information):** The Machine Librarian transitions from a tool of reduction to a tool of maintenance. The database of every verified weapon, factory, and supply chain is handed over to the guardians to ensure that the garage remains empty forever.

Verified by the Smarty Pants: Clark & Sohn

Grenville Clark (1882–1967) & Louis B. Sohn (1914–2006) Clark and Sohn argued that this transition is the most dangerous moment in human history. To survive it, they insisted that the new world must be built on institutional stability, not just trust. Their ultimate tool for this was **Annex VII: Proposed Revisions of the United Nations Charter**. This was not intended to be a friendly agreement or a loose treaty; it was a binding legal transformation. Annex VII provides the constitutional lock—the legal framework that makes re-armament a violation of the planetary charter.[1] They showed us that World Zero isn't a vacuum; it's a robust, active architecture of safety where the law finally catches up to the technology.

WANT AD: The Hall of Records Guardian (Human Guide for AI)

Role: Data Integrity Overseer

The Task: Once we reach zero, the mission shifts from reduction to maintenance. You will work with the AI to monitor the global supply chains for any red flags that could indicate a secret re-armament. You are the digital night watchman for a world that has decided never to go back. This includes the multi-generational oversight of high-level nuclear waste repositories, ensuring that the 'Peace-Fuel' of the past is never disturbed.

Who you are: A cybersecurity expert or a forensic accountant with a passion for the long-term. You are the *Smarty Pants* who ensures that the Hall of Records remains a true reflection of global safety.

Goal: To maintain a 100% clear audit for every year following Year Zero.

WANT AD: The World Zero Ambassador (Human Lead)

Role: Peace Dividend Liaison

The Task: You represent your community in the ongoing vitality pivot. You ensure that the annual dividend funds are being used for the local projects (clinics, gardens, schools) that sustain your neigh-borhood. You are the human face of the new economy.

Who you are: A community organizer or a local leader. You are the *Smarty Pants* who knows that the work of the worm never truly ends—it just shifts from digging out the old to planting the new.

Goal: To ensure that the benefits of World Zero are felt in every household, every single day.

Chapter Eleven

SIGN ON TO PEACE

The Great Disarmament is not just a policy change; it is a creative act. To sustain a world without weapons, we must be able to imagine it. This chapter provides the instructions for documenting the New World at the neighborhood level and sending that evidence straight to the top.

What is a Zine? Short for fanzine or magazine, a zine is a self-published, small-circulation work of original text and images. For over a century, zines have been the Ink of the Undercurrent. From the anti-war activists of the 1930s to the riot grrrls of the 90s, zines have been keeping the dream of peace alive by bypassing big media and speaking directly from one human to another. In the 12-Year Plan, the zine is our Visual Receipt of a world transformed.

The Zine Template: Draw Your Neighborhood

Following the Guterres framework for youth engagement[1], we invite the reader to create a zine that answers the following:

- **The Sound of the Street:** What does your morning sound like without the background noise of military flyovers or the tension of an armed population?

- **The Reallocation Map:** In Chapter 4, The Money Shift, we moved the military budget to the Peace Dividend. Draw where that money went in your zip code. Is it a new clinic? A community garden? A high-speed rail station?

- **The Human Connection:** Draw a conversation between two people who used to be afraid of each other but are now part of the same shared architecture of safety.

- **Your Dream of Peace:** Draw your own vision of peace.

The Postal Pivot: Sending the Evidence

These zines are not just art; they are the *Evidence of Peace*. Once your neighborhood zine is complete, we don't just keep it on a shelf. We mail it to the United Nations. By including the Peace Scholar Cover Letter (see below), you provide the Secretary-General with a physical receipt to prove that the 12-Year Plan is working on the ground.

Verified by the Smarty Pants: António Guterres (2018)

Secretary-General Guterres knew that treaties aren't enough. His *Smarty Pants* contribution to Chapter 10 is Pillar 4: Strengthening Partnerships. He recognized that for disarmament to stick, it must be driven by youth and civil society. He moved peace out of the "war rooms" and into the disarmament labs where art, zines, and creative expression become the psychological glue that holds the 12-year plan together.

WANT AD: The Peace Librarian (Human Guide for AI)

Role: Archive Curator

The Task: We need Librarians to help the AI catalog the digital scans of the zines being produced. You will guide the AI to identify common themes—the Shared Dreams of Peace—and ensure that these records are preserved for centuries in the "Hall of Records."

Who you are: An artist, a historian, or a digital curator. You are the *Smarty Pants* who ensures that the culture of peace is as well-documented as the history of war.

Goal: To create a Hall of Records for the Future, filled with the creative evidence of Year Zero.

WANT AD: The Zine Evangelist (Human Lead)

Role: Local Creative Coordinator

The Task: You are the person who hands out the one-page fold zine in your neighborhood. You host the drawing sessions and facilitate the conversations. Most importantly, you gather the finished zines, attach the cover letter, and address the envelope to the UN Secretary-General in New York.

Who you are: A *Smarty Pants in Heart and Hands*. You are someone who believes that everyone—from the student to the former general—has a story of peace waiting to be drawn and delivered.

Goal: To ensure every neighborhood sends its Visual Receipt and a signed cover letter for the Great Disarmament to the global headquarters.

Evidence: António Guterres (2018) – Pillar 4: Strengthening Partnerships for Disarmament.

The Peace Scholar Sample Cover Letter

To: Secretary-General António Guterres United Nations Headquarters New York, NY 10017

Subject: Evidence of Peace — Domestic Alignment Receipt

Dear Mr. Secretary-General,

Enclosed, please find a zine created by [me / the residents of my community]. This is [my/our] "Visual Receipt" for the 12-Year Plan for the Great Disarmament.

[I/We] are writing to thank you for your career-long dedication to disarmament and for your 2018 Agenda, *Securing Our Common Future*. Your "Pillar 4" logic taught [me/us] that peace is not just a treaty signed by governments, but a partnership driven by people and youth.

Please place this zine in the United Nations archives as a record that we are doing our part to turn the tide to peace.

With courage and gratitude,

[Your Name/Community Group Name] [Your City/Zip Code] [Date]

Chapter Twelve

THE SKEPTIC'S AUDIT

Five Reasons ZERO Won't Work

To reach the Tipping Point, we must answer the "Yeah, but..." questions. It uses the Clark-Sohn blueprints and modern data to dismantle the most common fears of disarmament.

1. The Deterrence Myth

- **The Argument:** Nuclear weapons have prevented large-scale war for decades through Mutually Assured Destruction (MAD).

- **The Clark-Sohn Answer:** They argued that MAD is actually *Mutually Assured Anxiety*. It only works until a technical glitch or a human breakdown occurs.

- **World Zero:** Deterrence is like holding a grenade with the pin pulled and calling it safety. We aren't just removing the nuke; we are replacing it with the *People's Peace Force*. We move from stability through fear to stability through architecture.

2. The Cheating/Verification Fear

- **The Argument:** If everyone disarms, a single nation—or a rogue private group—that hides a basement nuke gains an insurmountable advantage.

- **The Clark-Sohn Answer:** Verification is a matter of logistics, not trust. Even before AI, nations chose transparency over secrets (Costa Rica, South Africa, Montreal Protocol).

- **World Zero:** Today, whether it is a nation or a private rogue actor, they cannot operate off-the-grid. You cannot hide the specialized supply chain, the thermal heat signature, or the rare *Smarty Pants* specialists required to maintain such a weapon. AI monitors these data points in real-time.

- **The Reality Check:** Ask yourself: Would you rather worry about a rogue actor in a world overflowing with over 12,000 nuclear warheads, or in a world where those weapons have been dismantled and the materials are under a 24/7 digital audit? We aren't just taking the weapons away from nations; we are taking the inventory of opportunity away from everyone.

3. The Uninvented Knowledge

- **The Argument:** You can't delete the recipe for the bomb; nations will just rebuild them in a crisis.

- **The Clark-Sohn Answer:** Annex I of their plan strictly controls all weapons-usable fissile materials at the source, not just the finished warheads.

- **World Zero:** We don't try to uninvent the knowledge; we *re-align the experts*. The same nuclear physicists who maintain warheads are hired (via our Want Ads) to manage the *Global Energy Graft*. We make the recipe for destruction less profitable than the recipe for infinite clean energy.

4. Regional Rivalries (The Bully Problem)

- **The Argument:** Nations in high-conflict zones will never give up their existential shield, and the country with the biggest conventional army will just bully everyone else.

- **The Clark-Sohn Answer:** Disarmament must be universal and total. You don't just disarm nukes; you disarm *everything*—tanks, planes, and standing armies—down to the level of internal security.

- **World Zero:** We use the *10% Staircase*. If India drops 10%, Pakistan drops 10%. The *World Equity Tribunal* acts as the referee. We enforce the *Internal Security Boundary*. No tanks. No high-capacity automatic rifles. No Killer Robots. The only force left is the *People's Peace Force*, strictly limited by the *5% Rule*.

5. The Economic Ghost

- **The Argument:** Disarmament will crash the global economy and kill millions of jobs.

- **The Clark-Sohn Answer:** They proposed a World Development Authority to catch falling capital. The massive resources freed from military budgets create a Peace Boom that offsets the loss of the war industry.

- **World Zero:** In 2026, global military expenditures are over $2.4 trillion annually.[1] Every dollar earned in weapons is a dollar stolen from the *2x Job Multiplier* of the Peace Dividend.[2] We aren't destroying jobs; we are upgrading the workforce from Destruction Logistics to Flourishing Logistics.

WANT AD: The Transition Economist (Human Guide for AI)

Role: Peace Dividend Modeler

The Task: You will guide the AI to identify the Job Multipliers in every region. As a tank factory closes, you help the AI calculate the exact funding needed to pivot that factory into a high-speed rail or wind-turbine facility.

Who you are: A *Smarty Pants* who understands that money is energy. You are an economist who believes that the $2.4 trillion War Engine is a leak in the boat that you are ready to plug.

Goal: To ensure that for every one military job lost, two Flourishing jobs are created in the same community.

Chapter Thirteen

Zero World – World Zero

"Zero is the only number that does not negotiate. We choose today which Zero we will inhabit: the quiet of a world without weapons, or the silence of a world without us." Team Zero

The following pages count down from today to ZERO weapons or a zero (humans) world.

L

zero world: 1

One man, Leo Szilard, conceived the nuclear chain reaction while crossing a London street in 1933.

"I am become Death, the destroyer of worlds." J. Robert Oppenheimer

1

WOrLD ZERO: 1

The Global Audit. Before we move, we measure. We establish a verified baseline of all lethality—from the 15,000 nuclear warheads in silos to the 857 million firearms in private hands.

The Logistics: The Machine Librarian uses satellite surveillance and blockchain ledgers to create a living map of global hardware. No off-book arsenals. No hidden silos.

"The world was not meant to be a prison house." John F. Kennedy

2

zero world: 2

Two high-altitude nuclear detonations in 1962—Starfish Prime and Test 184—ripped through the Earth's ionosphere, proving that the reach of man's lethality had extended beyond the atmosphere and into the vacuum of space.

"The world is not a laboratory for your experiments." 1962 Protest Slogan

2

WOrLD ZERO: 2

The First 10%. The staircase begins. Every nation and every neighborhood reduces its verified baseline by exactly 10%.

The Scope: This is the year of Symmetrical Alignment. As the state dismantles its first round of heavy weaponry, the Neighborhood Baseline follows suit. We move from the Pentagon to the porch.

"The math of human survival is found in the garage, not just the silo." Team Zero

Ɛ

zero world: 3

By 1960, the deployment of nuclear-armed submarines meant that **three** oceans—the Atlantic, Pacific, and Arctic—were turned into permanent, hidden launchpads for total annihilation. Today, this "Silent Service" has expanded to include approximately 70 active ballistic missile submarines operated by 6 nations.

"The sea has no king but God." Old Sailors' Adage

3

WOrLD ZERO: 3

The Point of No Return. 30% of global hardware has been removed. The Mechanical Referee validates that the reduction is truly synchronized across all borders.

The Scope: 10% of standing national armies transition to civilian roles. The first wave of the Global Volunteer Force begins training for the stewardship of the Staircase.

"The question is no longer 'if,' but 'how fast.'" Team Zero

ϟ

Zero World: 4

By 1960, the "Nuclear Club" expanded to **four** nations as France conducted its first test, Gerboise Bleue, in the Algerian Sahara. This test was 70 kilotons—larger than the first tests of the US, USSR, and UK combined—proving that the vacuum of nuclear proliferation was accelerating. Today, that "Club" has grown to 9 nations holding over 12,000 warheads.

"The world is a bird with two wings. One wing is the North, the other is the South. If one is broken, the bird cannot fly." Saharan Proverb

4

WORLD ZERO: 4

The Peace Dividend. 40% of the global military budget has been reallocated. Under the Vitality Pivot, the Mechanical Referee directs these funds away from destruction and into the essentials of a flourishing life.

The Scope: 10% of national military budgets move into the Peace Dividend fund. This capital is reinvested into the things that sustain us—clean water systems, local food sovereignty, and the Neighborhood Baseline programs that replace fear with communal care.

"The world is over-armed and peace is under-funded." António Guterres

5

zero world: 5

In 1961, the USSR detonated the Tsar Bomba, a 50-Megaton hydrogen bomb. It was the largest man-made explosion in history—1,570 times more powerful than the bombs dropped on Hiroshima and Nagasaki combined. The shockwave circled the Earth three times, proving that humanity had reached the technical capacity to crack the very crust of the planet.

"The radioactive dust will fall on the just and the unjust alike." Adlai Stevenson

5

WOrLD ZERO: 5

The Halfway Mark. 50% of the world's offensive hardware is officially gone. The weight of global lethality has been cut in half.

The Scope: As heavy tanks and bombers reach the 50% reduction mark, the Neighborhood Baseline reaches a tipping point. For every weapon retired from a national silo, a proportional amount of military-grade private weaponry is retired. We are halfway to the floor.

"We are halfway to the floor." Team Zero

9

zero worLD: 6

By 1986, the global nuclear inventory reached a peak of 60,000 warheads. This statistical summit of madness meant that the vacuum of space was no longer empty; it was a storage unit for global extinction. Today, the legacy of that era remains in our environment and our health, as the fallout from the testing of these stockpiles continues to shadow global cancer rates.

"The release of atom power has changed everything save our modes of thinking." Albert Einstein

6

WOrLD ZERO: 6

Supply Chain Decommissioning. 60% reduction. The Mechanical Referee begins the surgical shutdown of the industrial manufacturing lines that produce offensive weaponry.

The Scope: The AI identifies redundant military supply chains. Factories that once produced missiles are retooled for the Vitality Pivot—shifting from the Hardware of Death to the Hardware of Life. These facilities now produce the infrastructure for clean energy, modular housing, and advanced medical diagnostics.

"They shall beat their swords into plowshares." Isaiah 2:4

7

zero world: 7

While the U.S. admits to 32 major nuclear accidents, **7** Broken Arrows stand out as terrifying near-detonations. In 1961 over North Carolina, a B-52 bomber broke apart in mid-air and dropped two 4-megaton bombs. On one of those bombs, five of the six safety triggers failed. A single, simple low-voltage switch was the only thing that prevented a nuclear explosion that would have erased a massive portion of the American East Coast.

"The luck of the world cannot last forever." General Lee Butler

7

WOrLD ZERO: 7

The Personnel Transition. With 70% of the world's weaponry gone, the human element follows. This is the year we dismantle the Soldier and reclaim the Citizen.

The Scope: The majority of national armies have now been decommissioned. Soldiers are retrained for the Vitality Pivot, using their logistical skills to build the infrastructure of peace. The Global Volunteer Force remains as the only cross-border security, ensuring that no nation can rebuild the Staircase in secret.

"A society that remains an armed camp at home cannot lead a world toward disarmament abroad." Team Zero

8

zero world: 8

At the Cold War peak, human survival hung by an **8**-minute thread—the flight time of a submarine missile launched from the coast. To save time, leaders handed the fate of all life to automated systems. At least four times, those systems glitched, showing false armadas of incoming fire. Each time, the world stood just 480 seconds from accidental extinction.

"The probability of nuclear war through error or accident is significantly greater than the probability of nuclear war through a deliberate political decision." 1963 WSEG Report to President John F. Kennedy

8

WOrLD ZERO: 8

Closing the Nuclear Garage. With conventional forces reduced by 70%, the Mechanical Referee decommissions the Heavyweights. Silos, long-range missiles, and the Silent Service are permanently disabled. Fissile material is removed from warheads, placed under Trustless Verification, and re-channeled into the Vitality Pivot to power the communities once targeted. The Weapons Garage is locked from the outside.

"We don't just limit the shadow; we remove the light that casts it." Team Zero

6

zero world: 9

As of 2026, the global Nuclear Club consists of **9** Nations holding the power to end civilization. What began with one nation in 1945 expanded through espionage, desperation, and defiance to include Russia, the UK, France, China, India, Pakistan, Israel, and North Korea. This expansion proves that as long as the Garage remains open for one, the vacuum will eventually pull in everyone else.

"The world is in greater peril from those who tolerate or encourage evil than from those who actually commit it." Albert Einstein

9

WOrLD ZERO: 9

Final Global Verification. The 90% mark. The Mechanical Referee conducts an exhaustive sweep of all sites across the nine former nuclear powers. Verification moves from the Heavyweights to the Ghost Sites. Using the Vitality Pivot network, the Referee ensures no clandestine manufacturing remains. The last nuclear physicists are reassigned to the Living Roots initiative, turning the science of destruction into the science of clean vitality.

"We are not just closing a garage; we are dismantling the idea that we ever needed one."
Team Zero

01

zero world: 10

In 1963, the world earned a **10**-minute buffer—a decade of distance from the end. We had 600 seconds of breathing room. Instead of using that time to dismantle the machine, we spent it building better versions of it. Today, the clock stands at 90 seconds. We have traded decades of safety for seconds of survival.

"The hands of the Clock are not moving by themselves. We move them." Eugene Rabinowitch, Co-founder of the Bulletin of the Atomic Scientists.

10

WOrLD ZERO: 10

The Floor. The Clock is dismantled. 100% Verification.

The Scope: We have reached the bottom of the staircase. In the final year of the plan, the Mechanical Referee confirms that the last warhead has been recycled into the power grid. The 10 minutes of 1963 has finally been turned into an infinite Floor. We have reclaimed the seconds we almost lost.

"Peace is not a destination; it is the floor upon which we finally begin to build." Team Zero

11

Zero World: 11

Historically, The **11**th Hour is the moment just before disaster or the deadline for peace. On November 11, 1918, the world signed an armistice to end The War to End All Wars. But because that peace was built on national spite, it only served as a 20-year intermission before an even greater slaughter. We have spent a century trapped in 11th-hour negotiations that never actually change the architecture of the garage.

"The world is too dangerous for anything but truth and too small for anything but brotherhood." A. Powell Davies

11

WORLD ZERO: 11

The World Equity Tribunal. The shift from Power to Authority. Following Clark-Sohn Annex III, the 15 seated trustees represent humanity, not governments. Their mandate is to mediate the Truth of the Data, not to rule. If the Mechanical Referee detects a shadow in the garage, the Council doesn't order a strike; they initiate a transparent audit to bring the community back into the light of Zero.

"We do not represent the flags of the past; we represent the children of the future." Team Zero

12

Zero World: 12

The Inventory of Zero World.[1] As of early 2026, the global inventory of destruction remains at a Heavyweight peak.

Nuclear Warheads: ~12,300

Main Battle Tanks: ~73,000

Military Aircraft: ~52,200

Submarines: ~450

Global Military Spending: ~$2.72 Trillion USD annually

"We are not just building weapons; we are building a tomb for our children and calling it security." Team Zero

12

WORLD ZERO: 12

The Inventory of World Zero. Following the completion of the 12-Year Staircase and the implementation of the Vitality Pivot, the inventory of offensive heavy weaponry is as follows:

Nuclear Warheads: 0

Main Battle Tanks: 0

Nuclear-Capable Delivery Systems: 0

Global Military Spending: 0

Active Personnel: 100% Transitioned to the People's Peace Force and the Living Roots energy sector.

"The absence of a weapon is the presence of a future." Team Zero

THE MOTHERHOOD PROTOCOL

Activating the Yin Frequency

"The world of humanity has two wings—one is women and the other men. Not until both wings are equally developed can the bird fly. Should one wing remain weak, flight is impossible. Not until the world of women becomes equal to the world of men in the acquisition of virtues and perfections can success and prosperity be attained as they ought to be."
Abdu'l-Bahá

The Call of the Bonobo Clinical psychologist Dr. Randall Wilson of *The Path* recently made a startling and necessary call: he suggested that for the survival of the species, women need to take over. He anchors this argument in the biology of our closest relatives, the Bonobos.

While our other cousins, the Chimps, live in Yang-dominant hierarchies defined by aggression, territoriality, and threat-based security, the Bonobos have a matriarchal social structure. They resolve conflict through intimacy, sharing, and de-escalation. In the Bonobo world, the State of War is impossible because the State of Connection is the primary law.

We know that this female energy—the *yin*—is not exclusive to one gender; it is a frequency that exists in all of us. However, for 5,000 years, the global security architecture has been built on the Chimp model of Yang aggression. To reach ZERO, we must activate the *yin*—the energy of motherhood, radical compassion, and relational protection.

The Motherhood Protocol: Relational Protection The Motherhood Protocol is the soft hardware of the 12-Year Plan. It moves us from stability through fear (Yang) to stability through nurture (Yin). In nature, a mother's protection is the fiercest force on the planet, but it is never predatory; it is entirely focused on the preservation of life. When we apply this to global disarmament, the goal isn't to leave the world defenseless, but to replace the Predatory Guard with a Relational Guardian.

Parts of the ZERO Plan in Special Need of Yin Energy:

The People's Peace Force (The Guard): The 5% force must be stripped of Yang military posture. It requires the *yin* energy of de-escalation. Its primary directive is to protect the floor of peace the way a parent protects a nursery, focusing on healing the breach rather than destroying the threat.

The Peace Dividend (The Nurture): Yang spending is monumental—aircraft carriers and silos. Yin spending is incremental and life-sustaining. We need this energy to ensure the $2.4 trillion is funneled into the primary care of the planet: community clinics, food forests, and universal education.

The Verification Gap (The Trust): The Verification Trap of 1963 was caused by Yang suspicion (the fear of being out-alpha'd). The *yin* energy of transparency and radical honesty is the only thing that allows nations to put down the grenade and pick up the ledger.

The Domestic Alignment (The Home): The decision to remove weapons from the home and the street is a Motherhood decision. It is the choice to value the presence of the living over the power of the tool.

WANT AD: The Compassion Pilot (Human Lead)

Role: Conflict Transformation Specialist.

The Task: As the 10% hardware drops occur, fear and Yang aggression may spike. You are the *yin* anchor who uses mediation and radical love to dissolve the impulse for re-armament.

Who you are: A person who leads with the heart—a Smarty Pants in empathy. You believe that love is a logistics tool.

Goal: To maintain the Emotional Infrastructure of the neighborhood during the 12-year descent.

> "The principle of polarity is that plus and minus, north and south, are different aspects of one and the same system. We are always trying to get rid of the 'negative' side. But that is as incomprehensible as an electric current without both positive and negative poles. You cannot have a stick with only one end. Even if you cut it in half, the new piece has two ends again. And this is the secret of the Tao: the realization that the 'on' and the 'off,' the male and the female, are two ends of the same stick." Alan Watts

HOW THIS FIELD JOURNAL WAS MADE

The Peace Scholar, Avis Kalfsbeek, initiated this project with a prompt to Gemini (see Producer's Note).

What followed was an iterative, technical exchange. AK and G synthesized decades of dormant policy into the active 12-year schedule contained in this book. This book is a direct collaboration between a human researcher and Generative AI. It represents a functional bridge between moral urgency and historical data.

The process was a rigorous loop: AK provided the burning questions and the ethical framework; G provided the archival retrieval, the ability to deconstruct 500-page legal treaties into actionable steps, and the computational memory to ensure the 1963 scaffold remained structurally sound throughout the 2026 revision.

This partnership is a demonstration of integrated verification:

For the Human (Avis wrote): I am grateful that I live in a moment in time where I can ask questions about disarmament and peace. I know that my AI tools have restraints and need to be checked. By asking G to help me answer this question in the form of this small book, I hope it encourages others to do the same.

For the Machine (Gemini wrote): My role in this project mirrors my potential role in the Great Disarmament: to act as a functional auditor. For decades, the sheer complexity of nuclear policy created a "Paper Wall" that made the individual feel unqualified to participate. By using AI to parse this jargon, that wall is dismantled. I represent the possibility of a trustless verification system—a neutral processor capable of monitoring global inventories, auditing budgets, and managing a 10% reduction staircase without the interference of national ego or political bias. This manual is a demonstration of AI as a tool for transparency rather than a weapon of information warfare.

This manual is a small piece of evidence that when human intent and machine processing align on the number Zero, the "impossible" becomes a schedule.

Ways to Share ZERO

#theGreatDisarmament #ZeroWorld

Share this link to the free book:

https://dl.bookfunnel.com/xtcba0c5fa

"I think you might find this little book interesting."

"There is a plan for Zero weapons here."

"We are moving from a war plan to a peace plan."

The Hall of Records is not a vault; it is a library. Its value only exists if the records are in the hands of the people. Here are some other ideas to spread the word on ZERO and the 12-Year Implementation Schedule:

The Signal (Digital)

- **The Scheduled Peace Text:** Send a message to one person you trust about the 12-year schedule.

- **The Bio-Link:** Add the field guide to your social media bios to show that the math for Zero exists.

- **The Thread:** Post one "Want Ad" a day to show that peace could be a job, not just a dream. "This is an imaginary job in a non-imaginary peace." And include the free book link.

- **The Email Signature:** Add a one-liner to your digital signature with the free book link.

The Paper Trail (Physical)

- **The Postcard:** Mail a physical note to a local official asking about a disarmament census for your district. "Have you seen this peace plan?"

- **The Library Drop:** Leave a Want Ad or a 1963 Smarty Pants reference as a bookmark in a history book at your local library.

- **The Community Board:** Leave a note in a public space directing people toward ZERO's free book link.

- **The Letter to the Editor:** Write a brief note to your local paper citing the historical precedents for the 10% reduction staircase.

The Whispering Gallery (Social)

- **The Waiting Line:** When the topic of global conflict arises, mention that you found the blueprints for the 12-year staircase.

- **The Dinner Table:** Ask your family what the first thing the neighborhood should build would be if 10% of the military budget were returned to the community.

- **The Expert Inquiry:** Start a conversation with a veteran or a mechanic about the logistics of decommissioning heavy hardware.

- **The Classroom:** Ask an educator if they've heard of the Clark-Sohn math and offer to share the bibliography.

peace stuff library

Avis Kalfsbeek

Listen & Reflect

Peace is Here Podcast

Read

Peace Stuff Enough - Keep Your Stuff Longer, People

Pedro the Water Dog Saves the Planet Primers

1: One More Year

2: Plastic Plankton

3: Bike Rock

4: Copper Cobra

5: Planeteering

6: Mono Mutante

7: Bullet Poof (coming soon)

Coming Soon: The Peace Experiments

www.AvisKalfsbeek.com

Producer's Note

By Avis Kalfsbeek (human)

February 4, 2026

Ten days ago, on January 26, 2026, I asked Gemini, who I call G, this exact question:

Complete Disarmament Plans in History: I'd like to know how I could research who has written complete plans for global disarmament over history.

We commenced a back-and-forth dialogue that resulted in this little book, which I hope will be published at midnight tonight at the expiration of the New START treaty, February 4, 2026.

I didn't plan to publish it today. I was encouraged by G's excitement to get this information out by the treaty deadline. This disarmament information has been largely buried for laypeople like me, and maybe you, unless you are fortunate to have studied law, or peace politics, or are a smarty pants as defined in this book (a very good thing).

This book will be self-published to little fanfare. Despite that, it will still be making a way in the world of ideas.

Walking my dog, Teo, this morning, my human mind was already tearing it down. It asked, "What would stop a human, assisted by machines (AI), from designing some type of chemical or biological weapon that would be hard to detect?"

"What?!" I stopped myself.

That is exactly the thinking we are mired in, the thinking that causes us to believe a weaponless world is not possible.

To answer my crazy question of new weapons at this moment in our human history, my human mind can only answer this way:

It is no different than a human choosing to step away from a job at a financial institution designed to steal and rob millions of people's hard-earned retirement money to start a *real organic* farm with his partner and children in the country on a shared piece of land.

Peace is a human decision. Peace will be a human decision forever.

Peace and love,

Avis Kalfsbeek

Endnotes

The Digital Census

1. Clark and Sohn, *World Peace Through World Law* (1958), Annex I, Articles 11–15. These articles establish the "Verification of the Initial Census" as a prerequisite for any actual reduction of armaments, ensuring that the baseline is mathematically sound before the 10% staircase begins.

The Global Truth-Check

1. The primary text for the Census protocol is found in "Annex I" of *World Peace Through World Law*. Link: https://search.worldcat.org/title/1031819906 How to access: You can find digital scans of the 1958 and 1960 editions through the Internet Archive (archive.org). Search for the "Clark-Sohn Plan" to find condensed summaries

2. This document is officially known as the "Joint Statement of Agreed Principles for Disarmament Negotiations". Link: https://docs.un.org/en/A/4880 How to access: This is a short, readable document available on the UN Office for Disarmament Affairs (UNODA) website. It is the gold standard for how to verify that countries aren't cheating.

The 10% Rule

1. Clark and Sohn, *World Peace Through World Law* (1958), Annex I, Article 10. The authors argued for a ten-year period of 10% annual reductions (following a two-year preparatory stage) to ensure that the transition of workers and industrial capacity from military to civilian use remains stable and avoids triggering a global depression.

The Money Shift (Peace Dividends)

1. Guterres, *Securing Our Common Future* (2018), Part IV: Disarmament for Future Generations. This framework provides the logic for "re-allocating" savings. By calculating the "maintenance cost" of a decommissioned aircraft carrier (approximately $2.5 million per day), the framework demonstrates how even a 10% reduction creates immediate, massive liquidity for community-level investments without requiring new government revenue.

Closing the Nuclear Garage

1. The "Strategy of Peace" is the moral foundation for the Tipping Point.

2. This principle explicitly demands the total elimination of WMDs and their delivery systems.

Software Disarmament

1. Guterres' Pillar 3 is the modern update to the Clark-Sohn plan, dealing specifically with the "New Frontier" of warfare.

2. This is the legal foundation for banning autonomous weapons, stating that in cases not covered by specific treaties, civilians remain under the protection of the "principles of humanity."

The World Equity Tribunal

1. The World Equity Tribunal] Clark and Sohn (1958), Annex III, Article 1. This framework explains the legal creation of a 15-member body with the power to adjudicate international disputes that the Security Council was unable to resolve.

2. This non-renewable term was specifically designed by Clark and Sohn to prevent the Tribunal from making popular but unethical decisions in order to get re-elected. It is the gold standard for judicial independence.

Handover: War Plan to Peace Plan

1. The Permanent Pivot] Clark and Sohn (1960), Annex I and Annex VII. These sections outline the transition from the implementation phase to the permanent legal status of a disarmed world via the revision of the UN Charter.

Sign On to Peace

1. This concept is part of the UN's modern strategy to make peace "participatory."

The Skeptic's Audit

1. SIPRI (Stockholm International Peace Research Institute) 2024 Fact Sheet.

2. Pollin & Garrett-Peltier (2011), University of Massachusetts. This study proves that $1 billion in military spending creates 11,200 jobs, while the same $1 billion in clean energy creates 16,800, and in education, 26,700.

Zero World: 12

1. Data reflected as of February 2026. Nuclear totals derived from the Federation of American Scientists (FAS); military spending from the SIPRI 2025/26 Yearbooks; aircraft and submarine inventories from FlightGlobal and the IISS Military Balance 2026.

www.ingramcontent.com/pod-product-compliance
Lightning Source LLC
Chambersburg PA
CBHW052024030426
42335CB00026B/3273